SPEAK LORD

FOR THY SERVANT

IS LISTENING

Conversations from God to his children

By: Gwen "Ms. Chocolate" Williams

The Lord is in His Holy Temple, let
all the earth keep silent before Him
Habakkuk 2:20

1

DEDICATION

This prayer journal was originally published for the Women on Mission group of the Franklin Avenue Baptist Church in New Orleans, La. as they prepared for their first mission trip. God moved mightily among all of us changing us into the women he wanted us to be. When Hurricane Katrina destroyed much of our "normal" lives, scattering us far from our dear church. We managed to remain in contact and remained doing missions.

Not only did this prayer journal make us stronger but added much to the spiritual growth of those who shared the journey with us. We, along with many others have been blessed by this book. Together we join in dedicating this reprint to Sis. Betty Larry who started the prayer renewal weekends with WMU.

As you start this 40-day prayer journal in silence, may you listen as God speaks. Your life will never be the same.

INTRODUCTION

To many of you who have known me over the years, you can testify I love to talk. My parents along with my schoolteachers gave me lots of spankings for talking too much. Daddy would always tell me: "Sis, you talk too much out your mouth." I took joy in dipping in grown folk business. No matter the subject, I just had to add my two-cents worth. I was blessed with the gift of talking.

Growing into intimacy with God I began to understand the importance of meditating and listening to God. Learning that prayer was a dialogue rather than a monologue. Most of my quiet times consisted of me fussing, crying, complaining, and pleading with God about what was bothering me. During those prayers of thanksgiving, I never gave God a chance to respond. It seemed as though prayer time was my time to say what I wanted to say never stopping to hear what God wanted to say. He has always brought something tragic to make me pause to hear him.

Many believers have a daily ritual of reading their bibles, meditating, and praying, but those times are usually one-sided. They have a little talk with Jesus and tell Him all about their troubles, but a few of us never sit and listen for His responses. That's what this journal is all about. I wrote it for my mission group, but I've adapted it for those desiring a word from God. As you begin this journey for the next 40 days of being alone with the father, plan on being still listening to His voice. As you begin your designated amount of time each day, find a quiet place, read the message and scripture verses, then remain silent for the rest of the time. Instead of you talking, just sit and quietly let the Father speak. When the time ends write what God said to you in the space provided. It's my prayer that this journal will bless you as much as it has blessed me.

Love, Ms. Chocolate

Day 1   I've got plans for you

Dear child, I know you usually spend time talking to me, but I want to spend these next few weeks talking to you. I have heard your cries and thoughts over the years, and I've enjoyed our times together. I have listened to you and have grown to love you even more than you know. Even when you thought I wasn't listening, I was. Now that you are ready to take this big step, I will continue to be there for you. I want you to know that being intimate with you is what I had in mind for us. Before you allowed me to come into your heart, I already had plans for your life. You are special to me and I will always love you. Even during the times when you felt undeserving of my love, I loved you and still had plans for you. Just be still, relax, and enjoy the journey.

Scriptures for today: *Jeremiah 29:11*
For I know the plans I have for you," declares the LORD, "plans to prosper you and not to harm you, plans to give you hope and a future.

God I hear you:

_____
_____
_____
_____
_____
_____
_____
_____
_____
_____
_____
_____
_____
_____
_____
_____
_____
_____
_____
_____
_____
_____
_____
_____
_____
_____

Day 2 Don't forget my access code

We've been talking together for a long time now and I know you know how to get in touch with me. I want to caution you about how the enemy, satan, will try to discourage and distract you from my presence. Remember it's his purpose to wiretap your prayers so my message doesn't reach you, but I have a special access code that locks him out. Remember when you asked Jesus into your heart and made him Lord? He is the only way to me. He travels between us via the Holy Spirit so that you will always be in constant communication with me. At the sound of that name JESUS, satan flees from your mind. Fill your thoughts with the words of my son and make sure he has a permanent place there. Be careful of anything that might cause static.

Scriptures for today: John 14:6 Jesus answered, "I am the way and the truth and the life. No one comes to the Father except through me. Phil. 2:5 In your relationships with one another, have the same mindset as Christ Jesus

God I hear you:

_____
_____
_____
_____
_____
_____
_____
_____
_____
_____
_____
_____
_____
_____
_____
_____
_____
_____
_____
_____
_____
_____
_____
_____
_____

Day 3   Yes, I called you

I know you must wonder just why I would choose you at this particular time in your life. You've got quite a few years on you and have thoughts of settling down to that comfortable lifestyle and just sit and wait for the rapture. You are wrong for I have more work for you to do. I have more children for you to share my love so they can become a part of my family. There are many in the world that need to know that I sent my Son to die for them so they may have eternal life. That's where you come in. Remember all those experiences you went through when you thought I had forgotten you? Well, I wanted you to have those experiences to make you stronger and bring you closer to me. How you came through your storm needs to be shared with those yet in the storm. Now is that time and I have chosen you. I need you to leave your comfort zone to take my message to the many uncomfortable places in the world so they may know of my love.

Scriptures for today: *Deut. 7:6 For you are a people holy to the LORD your God. The LORD your God has chosen you out of all the peoples on the face of the earth to be his people, his treasured possession.*
I Peter 2:9 *But you are a chosen people, a royal priesthood, a holy nation, God's special possession, that you may declare the praises of him who called you out of darkness into his wonderful light.*

God I hear you:

_____
_____
_____
_____
_____
_____
_____
_____
_____
_____
_____
_____
_____
_____
_____
_____
_____
_____

Day 4   Don't forget to put me first

I know you're already thinking about the journey before you and the things you are called to do. Perhaps you're thinking about what I'm saying to you as you prepare to share this experience. Many questions flood your mind but remember that it's my voice that is speaking. Remember the command to put me first and allow me to direct your steps. Even when satan attempt to block your path I will direct you over, though, and around them. This may sound weird to you but remember that I am a jealous God. I desire to have first place in your heart and first place on your journey. See I have all the plans and directions for your successful journey, but I need you to put your trust in me.

Scriptures for today: Pro. 3:4-5:
Trust in the LORD with all your heart and lean not on your own understanding; in all your ways submit to him, and he will make your paths straight.

Matt. 6:33: *But seek first his kingdom and his righteousness, and all these things will be given to you as well.*

God, I hear you:

_____
_____
_____
_____
_____
_____
_____
_____
_____
_____
_____
_____
_____
_____
_____
_____
_____
_____
_____
_____
_____
_____

Day 5   Start Packing

I know how excited you are to be my servant and you just can't wait to share what this experience has meant to you. Before you start your missionary journey, I want to make sure you pack some necessary items. First, I want you to reach for my word. My word has been around for lots of years and I've spoken to my children through those words from my heart. I realize some of my children take my word for granted. Many would rather admire them than obey them. When I chose you, I knew you would use my word as I intended. Remember my word is a light to guide you, a sword to convict you, an instruction manual to teach you my truths, and a comforter during trouble times. My word will STAND forever, and it will never change. Meditate on them day and night. Commit them to memory to use as a weapon against the enemy. Everything you need for the journey is in my word. Don't you ever leave without it.

Scriptures for today: Psalms 119:105
Your word is a lamp for my feet, a light on my path.
II Timothy 2:15 *Do your best to present yourself to God as one approved, a worker who does not need to be ashamed and who correctly handles the word of truth.*
II Timothy 3:16 *All Scripture is God-breathed and is useful for teaching, rebuking, correcting and training in righteousness.*

God I hear you:

_____
_____
_____
_____
_____
_____
_____
_____
_____
_____
_____
_____
_____
_____
_____
_____
_____

Day 6   Follow my lead

When my Son lived on the earth, he challenged many to deny themselves, take up the cross, and follow Him. Many accepted that challenge, sacrificed everything to meet that challenge. Those followers traveled many places leaving the mark of Christ on all who would believe. I am so glad that you have answered the challenge and I assure you that my spirit will be with you also. I know you could have chosen the world's path full of fame and fortune, but you decided to make me your choice. The road will not be easy, for the enemy has already set up roadblocks with lots of challenges. Many days will cause you to doubt and give up but remember that I am always with you. My Son came to the earth to provide you with footprints to follow. Jesus is the way, the truth, and the life.

Scriptures for today: *Matt. 4:19 "Come, follow me," Jesus said, "and I will send you out to fish for people."*
Matt, 28:19-20 *Therefore go and make disciples of all nations, baptizing them in the name of the Father and of the Son and*

of the Holy Spirit, [20] and teaching them to obey everything I have commanded you. And surely, I am with you always, to the very end of the age."

God, I hear you:

_____

_____

_____

_____

_____

_____

_____

_____

_____

_____

_____

_____

_____

_____

_____

_____

_____

_____

_____

Day 7 Take out the trash

I remember the day you confessed your sins and asked my Son to forgive you and come live in your heart. My heart rejoiced along with the angels and sang a hallelujah chorus just for you. Oh, the joy that flooded my soul to have you in my family. Salvation was just the beginning of growing into an intimate relationship with me. I want all of you not just to save you from hell, but to always be there for you. I want to be your Father to bless you and provide whatever you need. You see, I'm a jealous God and will not share you with anyone or anything else. You must rid yourself of the TRASH!!! I know you love those things and have become so attached to them, but they must go. It's tough, but I want to help you. I'm an expert at recycling trash so let me help you. I can take that trash away permanently, but you have to bag it.

Scriptures for today: *2 Chronicles 7:14 if my people, who are called by my name, will humble themselves and pray and seek my face and turn from their wicked ways, then I will hear from heaven, and I will forgive their sin and will heal their land.*

Hebrews 12:1-2 *Therefore, since we are surrounded by such a great cloud of witnesses, let us throw off everything that hinders and the sin that so easily entangles. And let us run with perseverance the race marked out for us, ² fixing our eyes on Jesus, the pioneer and perfecter of faith. For the joy set before him he endured the cross, scorning its shame, and sat down at the right hand of the throne of God.*

God, I hear you:

_____
_____
_____
_____
_____
_____
_____
_____
_____
_____
_____
_____
_____
_____
_____
_____

Day 8   My Praise

Oh, how I love it when my children sing praises and give glory in my name. When you come together with the family and sing, pray, preach, and worship; I love it! Can I be honest? All of heaven rejoices every time you worship. Do you ever wonder why I expect and love it when you give me praise? I need to know that you appreciate all that I do for you. I need to know that you are glad I sent Jesus to die for you. I never created you to be a computer to obey my every command. I loved you enough to have free will to make choices. When you praise me, I know you've made the right choice. Whenever your praises reach my heart, I send my blessings down to you. So, go ahead, lift your voice and let your praises ring.

Scripture for today: Psalms 100: *Shout for joy to the LORD, all the earth.*
Worship the LORD with gladness; come before him with joyful songs.
Know that the LORD is God. It is he who made us, and we are his; we are his people, the sheep of his pasture.

Enter his gates with thanksgiving and his courts with praise; give thanks to him and praise his name. For the LORD is good and his love endures forever, his faithfulness continues through all generations.

God, I hear you

_____
_____
_____
_____
_____
_____
_____
_____
_____
_____
_____
_____
_____
_____
_____
_____
_____
_____
_____
_____
_____
_____
_____
_____
_____
_____
_____
_____
_____

Day 9   My Presence

I am so in love with you that I always want you to be in my presence. I am jealous for you and I refuse to share you with anyone or anything. You belong to me, I created you to be totally committed to me. Nobody can ever replace me in your life. It's important that you stay in my presence because the enemy if constantly trying to harm you. When you're in my presence I can protect you from whatever the enemy throws your way. I can lead you through unknown paths without straying. I can keep you from falling into temptation. I can provide everything you need to live the abundant life. It is my pleasure to love you and to bless you.

Scripture for today: Psalms 16:11
You will show me the path of life; In Your presence is fullness of joy; At Your right hand are pleasures forevermore. (NKJV)

God I hear you:

_____
_____
_____
_____
_____
_____
_____
_____
_____
_____
_____
_____
_____
_____
_____
_____
_____
_____
_____
_____
_____
_____
_____
_____
_____
_____

Day 10   My Power

I am so proud of you and how you have grown since you gave me your heart. I've watched you in Sunday School, Bible Study, and during those quiet times of personal meditation. I know you enjoy attending worship service along with your family just to give me glory. These are powerful experiences, but please don't forget my power. Before Jesus left the earth, he promised to send another comforter: The Holy Spirit. That's my power that lives within. That's how I manifest myself with your heart. You can't see me, but you can feel me and know that I'm there. As you face the many fiery darts the enemy throws your way, my power will see you through. As you study doubts and fears will seek to deter you, but my power will assist you into growing stronger as my child.

Scriptures for today: Acts 1:8 But you will receive power when the Holy Spirit comes on you; and you will be my witnesses in Jerusalem, and in all Judea and Samaria, and to the ends of the earth."

Zech. 4:6 *This is the word of the L*ORD *to Zerubbabel: 'Not by might nor by power, but by my Spirit,' says the L*ORD *Almighty.*

God I hear you:

_____
_____
_____
_____
_____
_____
_____
_____
_____
_____
_____
_____
_____
_____
_____
_____
_____
_____
_____
_____
_____

Day 11   My Provisions

I understand that most of our times together you talk to me about your needs. I see you struggle trying to make ends meet with the little you earn. I know you work hard to help support your family, but every day there's a need that was not in the budget. You make promises that you have no idea how to keep them. You wish you could do more to provide for your family, but your resources are limited. I see your faith every month when you give your tithes, but I also know how worried you are. I want you to depend totally upon me to provide for you, but I need you to trust me. LISTEN!!!

I know the needs you have even before you ask. You are my child and I will never let you go without what you need. I love you. You have got to trust me as you walk by faith. Quit being so impatient and let me supply your every need. Trust me to decide when it's time to shop at Saks or buy that BMW.

Scriptures for today: Psalms 23:1
The LORD is my shepherd, I lack nothing.
Phil. 4:19 *And my God will meet all your needs according to the riches of his glory in Christ Jesus.*

God I hear you:

_____
_____
_____
_____
_____
_____
_____
_____
_____
_____
_____
_____
_____
_____
_____
_____
_____
_____
_____

The world I created is filled with turmoil and strife that I hardly recognize it. There are days I am so angry at what the enemy has done to my children and my beautiful world. That's why I sent my Son to go down there and show my children how to live in all the mess. One of the benefits you enjoy being part of the family is my peace. I know you are plagued by the enemy at your job, in your neighborhood and among your family members. But, in the midst of all that the enemy throws at you, I want you to enjoy my peace. Satan is trying to confuse your mind and fill it with worry, but I want you to fill it with my peace. I know how you are stressed out and want to fuss or strike back, but just wait on me to handle the enemy. I have plans for him. My peace will carry you through the storms of life. It's a free gift from me to serve as a testimony to others who yet struggle in the storm.

Scriptures for today: Isa. 26:3 *You will keep in perfect peace those whose minds are steadfast, because they trust in you.*

John 14: 27 *Peace I leave with you; my peace I give you. I do not give to you as the world gives. Do not let your hearts be troubled and do not be afraid.*

God I hear you:

_____

_____

_____

_____

_____

_____

_____

_____

_____

_____

_____

_____

_____

_____

_____

_____

_____

_____

_____

_____

Day 13   My Protection

It was my intention to create a perfect world where my children would live in peace and harmony. My beautiful world was destroyed by the enemy so that many of you are afraid to go and share my word. Fear has entered your thoughts and has caused you to doubt that I would always be with you as I promised. I will protect you wherever you go and whatever you do in my name. The enemy uses deception through lies to keep you locked inside so lost ones will never know my truth. I know your fears and that you feel like hiding out until I return, but that's not of me.

Remember how I protected my servants in the bible? I promised to always be there to deliver them during difficult times. There is nothing that can happen to you that I cannot provide a way out. That's one of the benefits of salvation. Jesus intercedes for you and he will always be a fence around you to protect you. You must move as I command and not by your own will. When you are led by my spirit, you have nothing to fear. Reach out to those needing a hug, a meal, a place to live, those in prison, those sick, and especially to those who are lost.

Scriptures for today: Exodus 14:14
The LORD will fight for you; you need only to be still.
2Timothy 1:7 *For God has not given us a spirit of fear, but of power and of love and of a sound mind. (NKJV)*

God I hear you:

_____
_____
_____
_____
_____
_____
_____
_____
_____
_____
_____
_____
_____
_____
_____
_____
_____
_____

Day 14   My Promise

I know you understand how many promises made to you have been broken. People you trusted ended up hurting your feelings. You may have made promises to me that you failed to follow through. I know. I understand that you're still growing. That relationship will take a while to become what I want it to be. You will grow more as you allow the Holy Spirit to reign in your life. While you are becoming, I want you to be confident that my promises are real. I always keep my word. When the enemy tries to deceive you, just remember my precious promises from my word. Every step taken is ordered by me and I place you in the center of my will all the time. I am always with you wherever you go. I will never lie to you therefore you can trust me to do what I say I will do. Nothing happens to you that is a surprise to me. I keep my promises and you can stand on them.

Scriptures for today: Joshua 1:9 *Have I not commanded you? Be strong and courageous. Do not be afraid; do not be*

*discouraged, for the LORD your God will be
with you wherever you go."*
I Corinthians 15:58 *Therefore, my beloved
brethren, be steadfast, immovable, always
abounding in the work of the Lord,
knowing that your labor is not in vain in the
Lord.*

God I hear you:

_____
_____
_____
_____
_____
_____
_____
_____
_____
_____
_____
_____
_____
_____
_____
_____
_____
_____
_____

Day 15   My Persistence

You remember the pain you felt when you were rejected by someone you thought loved you? You trusted this person with your heart, and they tossed it around like a ball. I felt that hurt as I watched you try to make it go away. As hard as you tried that relationship ended leaving you alone and depressed. I put my strong arms around you and let you cry it out as I dried your tears. In my arms you found strength to pick up the pieces and keep going. Now that you are strong enough to share what I did for you, satan will constantly remind you of your past failures. You must remind him of his future and press on. Just as I kept pursuing you until you gave me your heart, I want you to keep pressing on to. Never give up until you reach your goal and I will always be with you. I know you're not a finished product, but I'm willing to stick with you until you become all I've created in you. Yes, there will be days I will have to chastise you, but my mercy is unlimited. My grace has brought you this far and my grace will lead you on.

Scriptures for today: Lamen. 3: 22-23
Because of the LORD's great love we are not consumed, for his compassions never fail.
They are new every morning; great is your faithfulness.
Isaiah 40: 31 *but those who hope in the LORD*
  will renew their strength. They will soar on wings like eagles;
  they will run and not grow weary; they will walk and not be faint.

God, I hear you:

_____

_____

_____

_____

_____

_____

_____

_____

_____

_____

_____

_____

_____

_____

_____

_____

_____

Day 16   Junk Food

As you are maturing, I've noticed that you are being careful what you put into your body. I'm so proud of you that you finally understand that your body is my temple and you need to be careful of the junk food. You must understand that I created those unhealthy delicacies to enjoy in moderation, not to abuse them. I see you attacking food like a long-lost buddy consuming it like your last meal. As your body ages it would not tolerate even the finest of my creations. I never intended for you to be unhealthy, constantly attacked by diseases because of your unhealthy choices. I'm sad that you have to deal with the consequences. But I'm still in the forgiving business and full of grace just for you. You also need to be careful how you feed your spiritual body, allow it to be consumed with junk food. You must always feed on my word, my truth, and my wisdom as you grow into a matured disciple.

Scriptures for today: James 1:21
Therefore, get rid of all moral filth and the evil

that is so prevalent and humbly accept the word planted in you, which can save you.
I Cor. 6:19-20 *Do you not know that your bodies are temples of the Holy Spirit, who is in you, whom you have received from God? You are not your own; you were bought at a price. Therefore, honor God with your body.*

God, I hear you:

_____
_____
_____
_____
_____
_____
_____
_____
_____
_____
_____
_____
_____
_____
_____
_____
_____
_____
_____

Day 17   I'm on Your Side

As a believer, you have days when you feel all alone thinking I've forgotten you. Even though you're surrounded by family and friends, you still feel alone. That's why it is important for you to know that I am always on your side. No matter what you do, I will always be on your side. There's no place you can go where I am not present. I created you and I know all about you. I know your every move and how you're going to react in every situation. That's why I wanted to live in your heart so you would experience my spirit. It is my good pleasure to bless you, to guide you, to love you, to watch over you, to dry your tears, to comfort you, to forgive you, and to bring you home to live with me forever.

Scriptures for today: Isa. 54:17 *no weapon forged against you will prevail, and you will refute every tongue that accuses you. This is the heritage of the servants of the LORD, and this is their vindication from me,"* *declares the LORD.*

Romans 8: 31 *What, then, shall we say in response to these things? If God is for us, who can be against us?*

God, I hear you:

_____

_____

_____

_____

_____

_____

_____

_____

_____

_____

_____

_____

_____

_____

_____

_____

_____

_____

_____

_____

_____

Day 18 Watch Out!!

Many times, I've watched you fall into the traps set for you by the enemy simply because you were not watching. I kept my promise to always be there to lead, guide, and direct your paths, but I gave you eyes to look where you were going. I gave you a mind and wisdom to discern the tricks of the enemy. You have five senses to learn my truths and apply them to your daily living. I have watched you being defeated by the enemy when I tried to warn you. It broke my heart to watch you suffer because you would not heed my warnings. You just would not listen.

I still love you and are proud of your spiritual growth. Now that you are growing, be careful to watch and pray in all situations. I am always with you, but I work through you. Remember to put on the whole armor I left for you to stand against the enemy. Remember as I sent my disciples as lambs among wolves, so send I you. Be wise as a snake yet gentle as a dove.

Scriptures for today: Mark 14: 38 *Watch and pray so that you will not fall into temptation. The spirit is willing, but the flesh is weak.*
I Cor. 16: 13-14 *Be on your guard; stand firm in the faith; be courageous; be strong.* *14 Do everything in love.*

God, I hear you:

Day 19   Shopping Spree

I created you with the gift to shop so I know how you love to go shopping. I have observed you spending hours checking out what's on same being a good steward of the money I give you. I know you keep the Mall in business. I was there watching you fight for the last sale item making sure you grab that last bargain. You love to shop. Well, I also have a storehouse full of bargains for you. Room after room is loaded with blessings, filled with rows and rows of gifts, racks filled with clothes of righteousness, boxes of precious promises, cases of the finest garments of praise, and out back I have the cattle on a thousand hills. In my storehouse you will never worry about running out of any particular item for I am over-stocked. You won't need cash or a credit card for all my merchandise is not for sale. It's been purchased just for you. All my merchandise comes with free delivery service. The only requirement is you have to show up and Ill let you shop and shop and shop and shop.

Scriptures for today: Gal. 5:22-23 *But the fruit of the Spirit is love, joy, peace, forbearance, kindness, goodness, faithfulness, gentleness and self- control. Against such things there is no law.*
Psalms 24:5 *They will receive blessing from the LORD and vindication from God their Savior.*

God, I hear you:

_____
_____
_____
_____
_____
_____
_____
_____
_____
_____
_____
_____
_____
_____
_____
_____
_____
_____
_____

Day 20   Sight Seeing

I gave James Weldon Johnson the gift to capture exactly my thoughts when I created the world. One day I stepped out on space and created the world. I hollowed out every valley and shaped every mountain. I spat out the seven seas, forming every tree covering the earth with such beauty and robbed each hillside with the finest flowers. Just to look at my creations is breath-taking even for me. Picking up a lump of clay, I blew into man my breath of life and he became a living soul. You were my finest creation and I love you jealously. I created this world, but I have a more beautiful home for you where you will live forever with me. Enjoy my creations on earth and make sure you take care of what I created, but don't get comfortable. Every now and them I will give you a foretaste of Heaven so you will get home sick.

Scriptures for today: Col. 3:2 *Set your minds on things above, not on earthly things.*

I Thess. 4: 17-18 *After that, we who are still alive and are left will be caught up together with them in the clouds to meet the Lord in the air. And so, we will be with the Lord forever.* [18] *Therefore encourage one another with these words.*

God, I hear you:

_____
_____
_____
_____
_____
_____
_____
_____
_____
_____
_____
_____
_____
_____
_____
_____
_____
_____
_____
_____

Day 21   Living Water

Water is good for the body and it aids in the proper functioning of many organs. I created water to sustain life while on earth. You are blessed to live in a country where you have access to clean water in abundance. As you travel you may encounter situations where the water is unsafe for drinking. Perhaps you will understand how it feels to be thirsty with no clean water available. You may even encounter persons too sick to drink for themselves and you will have to help them drink. Maybe you will work in a disaster area where the water source has been destroyed and you have to drive the water truck. There are many mission areas that need wells to be dug so the villagers won't have to walk miles for water. These situations refer to physical water, but not the kind of water that I offer to my family. One taste of my living water and you will never thirst again. As you travel be sure to take along some of my living water to those with thirsty souls.

Scriptures for today: Isaiah 12:3 *With joy you will draw water*
*   from the wells of salvation.*
John 4:10-14 *Jesus answered, "Everyone who drinks this water will be thirsty again, but whoever drinks the water I give them will never thirst. Indeed, the water I give them will become in them a spring of water welling up to eternal life."*

God, I hear you:

_____

_____

_____

_____

_____

_____

_____

_____

_____

_____

_____

_____

_____

_____

_____

_____

_____

Day 22   True Praise

What a day!!! I wished you could have been there to see my Son come riding into the city. Such a grand occasion fitting for a king. Of course, I knew this crowd would be the same crowd that would yell "Crucify Him" later that same week. Their praise didn't last too long for it was just a show for one day. I see a difference in you because you have my spirit with your heart. You know how to worship me from your heart. True praise comes when you worship me with your mind, soul, and with your whole heart. I appreciate true praise from my family when they express thanks for all I have done for them. I welcome your praise when you give glory and honor to me as the King of Kings and the Lord of Lords. I am the Great I Am, The Everlasting Father, the Prince of Peace, never forget to give me True Praise!!!

Scripture for today: Psalms 150
Hallelujah! Yes, praise the Lord! Praise him in his Temple and in the heavens, he made with mighty power.! Praise him for his mighty works. Praise his unequaled greatness. Praise him

with the trumpet and with lute and harp. Praise him with the drums and dancing. Praise him with stringed instruments and horns. Praise him with the cymbals, yes, loud clanging cymbals. Let everything alive give praises to the Lord! You praise him! Hallelujah! (TLB)

God, I hear you:

_____

_____

_____

_____

_____

_____

_____

_____

_____

_____

_____

_____

_____

_____

_____

_____

_____

_____

_____

Day 23   Good Seeds

You were created in my image as I blew into you the breath of life. When I commanded you to go replenish the earth, you became my good seeds. I so looked forward to watching you grow producing a family that I could love. Oh, how I long for a family that I could have sweet fellowship with. It grieved my spirit as satan tempted you to disobey my commands. I came to earth as Jesus to rescue you from the grip of the enemy so you could once again grow and produce good fruit. Please don't ever forget that you are mine because I created you and redeemed you from the hands of the enemy. I have commissioned you to go forth throughout the earth and make disciples. You are to continue planting seeds. Just plant the seen and let me do the rest. The spirit within you produces the seeds of love, kindness, joy, faith, peace, hope, forgiveness, and patience. Everywhere you go plant these seeds and you will bear much fruit.

Scripture for today: Matt 13: 3-9

3 Then He spoke many things to them in parables, saying: "Behold, a sower went out to sow. 4 And as he sowed, some seed fell by the wayside; and the birds came and devoured them. 5 Some fell on stony places, where they did not have much earth; and they immediately sprang up because they had no depth of earth. 6 But when the sun was up, they were scorched, and because they had no root they withered away. 7 And some fell among thorns, and the thorns sprang up and choked them. 8 But others fell on good ground and yielded a crop: some a hundredfold, some sixty, some thirty. 9 He who has ears to hear, let him hear!" (NKJV)

God, I hear you:

_____

_____

_____

_____

_____

_____

_____

_____

_____

_____

_____

_____

Day 24 Deep Roots produce Good Fruit

The day you joined my family it was my desire that you produce good fruit. It's been my joy to live in your heart to guide you along the way. I've watched you study my word and apply them to your life. I've enjoyed the sweet times of fellowship during worship. I've held you in my arms as you poured out your heart and allowed me to love you through the most difficult days. I loved the way you reached out to me for guidance when the way got rough. Many times, on the path you felt like giving up when you lost strength to fight the enemy. During those days you allowed me to carry you until you were strong enough to go on. When I see you now, all grown up, ready to blossom into my woman, my heart rejoices. Those growing pains were tough, but they made you stronger allowing your roots to go deeper in my ways. May you continue to grow deeper and produce more fruit.

Scriptures for today: Eph. 3:18 *may have power, together with all the Lord's holy people, to grasp how wide and long and high and deep is the love of Christ,*
Col. 2:6-7 *So then, just as you received Christ Jesus as Lord, continue to live your lives in him, 7 rooted and built up in him, strengthened in the faith as you were taught, and overflowing with thankfulness.*

God, I hear you:

_____
_____
_____
_____
_____
_____
_____
_____
_____
_____
_____
_____
_____
_____
_____
_____
_____

I'm so proud of you especially how you are taking care of your physical body. I see you at the gym working out and trying out all those nutritious smoothies. It is important that you keep your physical body in shape as you prepare to do my will. Yes, you need to be physically healthy to serve me, but you also need to spiritually healthy as well. Just as you are careful about what you eat physically, you are to be careful to feed your spirit. People may be drawn to your outside appearance, but what's inside can change the people you witness to. Just as you exercise your physical body, don't forget to exercise your spiritual body. Read and meditate on my word daily. Seek spiritual things and worship with other like-minded believers. Don't forget that I am your coach forever.

Scripture for today: I Cor. 9:24-27
24 Do you not know that in a race all the runners run, but only one gets the prize? Run in such a way as to get the prize. 25 Everyone who competes in the games goes into strict training. They do it to get a

crown that will not last, but we do it to get a crown that will last forever. **26** *Therefore I do not run like someone running aimlessly; I do not fight like a boxer beating the air.* **27** *No, I strike a blow to my body and make it my slave so that after I have preached to others, I myself will not be disqualified for the prize.*

God, I hear you:

_____
_____
_____
_____
_____
_____
_____
_____
_____
_____
_____
_____
_____
_____
_____
_____
_____
_____
_____

Day 26   Shine your Light

The world I created was filled with my light, but satan stole some of the light and created spaces of darkness. As my child I am calling you to go to those dark places and let your light shine. Remember when you first got saved and all you had was a tiny flicker, but as you grew the brighter your light became. Everywhere you go that little light keep on shinning. If the world is ever to know about me it will come from that light within you. I don't need preaching rocks, but messages from those with strong lights to dispel the darkness. Through you the world will feel the warmth of my love, so you've got to let your light shine all the time. Don't let satan blow it out so make sure you are keeping your lamps filled and wicks trimmed.

Scripture for today: Matt. 5:16 *In the same way, let your light shine before others, that they may see your good deeds and glorify your Father in heaven.*

58

God, I hear you:

_____
_____
_____
_____
_____
_____
_____
_____
_____
_____
_____
_____
_____
_____
_____
_____
_____
_____
_____
_____
_____
_____
_____
_____
_____
_____
_____
_____

Day 27   **Binding Love**

Talking about love is one of my favorite subjects especially since I created it. It was love that moved me to create the world. Love motivated me to create you and provide a place for you in my beautiful world. It was love that caused me to love you even when you chose to be disobedient. When I came to earth and became the perfect sacrifice for your sins, shedding my blood was all because of love. You are a product of my unconditional love. You and I are forever bonded by my love which will never change. Because of my love for you I want you to show this same love to your sister. As you travel in the world let my love flow through you. This is the only way to draw others into a relationship with me.

Scriptures for today: Romans 5: 8
But God demonstrates his own love for us in this: While we were still sinners, Christ died for us.
I Cor. 13:4-6 *4Love is patient, love is kind. It does not envy, it does not boast, it is not proud. 5It does not dishonor*

others, it is not self-seeking, it is not easily angered, it keeps no record of wrongs. ⁶Love does not delight in evil but rejoices with the truth.

God, I hear you:

_____

_____

_____

_____

_____

_____

_____

_____

_____

_____

_____

_____

_____

_____

_____

_____

_____

_____

_____

_____

Day 28   Blind Faith

I have the hardest time trying to get you to understand what faith is. I said a lot about faith in my word, but I don't think you get it. Yes, I want to you live by faith putting all your trust in me, but that does not mean quit your job, sell the house, give away all your money and clothing, and leave your family to follow me. What I said was to put your trust in me not in material things. I want you to live abundantly because that's how I chose to bless you. I never intended for those things to hinder you from doing my will. I want you to be available to go when I call without thinking about what you are giving up following me. Don't question my plans just trust me to do my will in you. I love you and I will always be with you.

Scriptures for today: Heb. 11:6 *And without faith it is impossible to please God, because anyone who comes to him must believe that he exists and that he rewards those who earnestly seek him.*

God, I hear you:

Day 29   Walking Worthy

Following me is a step-by-step process as directed by my Spirit. You do not move on your on, but rather guided according to my will. Just as I have made plans for you, I also order your steps. You cannot make one step without my knowledge of where you're going and why. Many times, you have wandered away from my will and I have to pull you back on course. Remember those old saints who walked with me and learn from their example. I want to use you to impact the world, but you must be careful how you walk. Your walk must match your talk. This is an impossible task for any human, but with me in control you can do it. Follow the footprints left by my Son and keep your eyes dead ahead on me.

Scriptures for today: Psalms 37:23 *The steps of a good man are [a]ordered by the LORD, And He delights in his way.*
I Peter 2:21 *For to this you were called, because Christ also suffered*

*for us, leaving us an example, that you
should follow His steps.*

God, I hear you:

_____
_____
_____
_____
_____
_____
_____
_____
_____
_____
_____
_____
_____
_____
_____
_____
_____
_____
_____
_____
_____

Day 30   I'm Alive

I love it when my family celebrates Easter even though for some it's about bunnies and fashions. When my children come together their celebration is about my Son you conquered death so that the world may know that I am GOD! He rose with all power in his hands so that all who believe in him would be free from the control of the enemy. Every Easter praises ring from every church declaring that their God LIVES!!

It grieves my spirit when some worship a dead god whose bones still lie in a grave. Yes, Jesus was buried, but his bones are not there for HE IS ALIVE!!!! Because he lives all who have placed their trust in him can face anything satan throws at them. Because Jesus lives, they have no fear about tomorrow and their life is worth living. As you worship today just rejoice knowing that once again, I have chosen you to GO and tell the world that: "I AM ALIVE!!!!

Scripture for today: John 20: 19-23 *On the evening of that first day of the week, when*

66

*the disciples were together, with the doors
locked for fear of the Jewish leaders, Jesus
came and stood among them and
said, "Peace be with you!"* [20] *After he said this,
he showed them his hands and side. The
disciples were overjoyed when they saw the
Lord. Again, Jesus said, "Peace be with
you! As the Father has sent me, I am sending
you." And with that he breathed on them and
said, "Receive the Holy Spirit. If you forgive
anyone's sins, their sins are forgiven; if you do
not forgive them, they are not forgiven."*

God, I hear you:

_____

_____

_____

_____

_____

_____

_____

_____

Day 31   *Speechless*

My precious child I love you so much especially the time we spend together. I love having you in my presence for I know our relationship grows stronger and stronger. I understand how difficult these times have been different especially since you are accustomed to doing all the talking. I look forward to hearing from you again, but during this special time I have so much of my truths that I want to share with you. The world is moving farther and farther from my design and it will become more difficult for you. That old enemy of mine is about to do many evil deeds and I want to make sure you are prepared for the warfare. I want you to be secure in what I've assigned you to do. I want you to be rooted and grounded in my word so there's do doubt that I live in you. Be prepared physically and spiritually to meet every challenge and don't forget the I am with you always. I have thoroughly enjoyed these last few days we have spent together.

Scriptures for today: Hab. 2:20
The LORD is in his holy temple;
let all the earth be silent before him.
Acts 15:12 The whole assembly became silent as they listened to Barnabas and Paul telling about the signs and wonders God had done among the Gentiles through them.

God, I hear you:

_____
_____
_____
_____
_____
_____
_____
_____
_____
_____
_____
_____
_____
_____
_____

Day 32   *My servant*

    When I called you and placed my spirit within your heart, you became my servant. I desire that you serve with a servant's heart and a servant's attitude. The world is filled with those less fortunate without what they need to live abundantly. Many are unloved beyond the reach of those willing to look beyond their faults to see their needs. The world offers many social programs that provide what they need physically, but I need you to go and meet their spiritual needs as well. I want you to go into the trenches where those who are ignored live to bring them living water so they will never thirst again. Remember when Jesus washed the disciple's feet, he challenged them to do likewise. I am offering you a towel as you go. You may not wash any feet, but you may dry a tear, wash a face, wrap a wound, clean a dish or just give it away. Whatever you do, do it in my name as my servant.

Scripture for today: Deut. 15:11
For there will never cease to be poor people in the land; that is why I am

70

commanding you, 'Open your hand willingly to your poor and needy brother in your land.' (CSB)
Mark 10:44 *and whoever wants to be first must be slave of all. For even the Son of Man did not come to be served, but to serve, and to give his life as a ransom for many."*

God, I hear you:

_____
_____
_____
_____
_____
_____
_____
_____
_____
_____
_____
_____
_____
_____
_____
_____
_____
_____
_____
_____

Day 33   Just Me

How I have treasured these days with you. Each precious moment spent alone with you in my presence has made you stronger. You have grown more and more to be like me. That was my purpose in creating mankind from the beginning. I wanted to have a special relationship, one that would last forever. I wanted man to enjoy fellowshipping daily with me. I wanted our spirits to join so that man would experience intimacy with me like no other relationship. One of my children refers to that kind of intimacy as a place of "farther still."

You have been a challenge and I have demanded that you give up everything meaningful to allow me to have dominion in your life. So many things and persons in your life were hard to give up and I had to remove them from you. I watched you cry, but then you came to understand I knew what was best. I'm amazed at the person you have become.

Scripture for today: Psalms 62: 1-2 *I am at rest in God alone;
my salvation comes from Him. He alone
is my rock and my salvation, my
stronghold; I will never be shaken.
(HCSB)*

God, I hear you:

_____
_____
_____
_____
_____
_____
_____
_____
_____
_____
_____
_____
_____
_____
_____
_____
_____
_____
_____

It breaks my heart to watch the enemy trap you and try to keep you in bondage. I grieve when you make wrong choices that also leads to bondage. I want you to know I have heard you cries for deliverance. It grieves my spirit when you wander off searching for freedom in all the wrong places. I know your struggle with bad relationships, bad financial habits, past mistakes, worrying about your future and trying to handle everything by yourself. I want you to understand my purpose in sending my Son to earth was to set men free. The freedom I give is real for I will never put you in bondage ever. I want you to live free and enjoy being free and never allow the enemy to place you in bondage again,

Scriptures for today: Isa. 61:1 *The Spirit of the Sovereign* LORD *is on me, because the* LORD *has anointed me to proclaim good news to the poor. He has sent me to bind up the brokenhearted, to proclaim freedom for the captives and release from darkness for the prisoners*

John 8:36 *So if the Son sets you free, you will be free indeed.*

God, I hear you:

_____
_____
_____
_____
_____
_____
_____
_____
_____
_____
_____
_____
_____
_____
_____
_____
_____
_____
_____
_____
_____
_____
_____
_____

Day 35 The Passover

Spending time along with you each day has made our relationship stronger. I hope you know that I have already gone ahead of you to put my plans in place. Because of our special time together, you are prepared to me the challenges that lie ahead. Before my Son was to be crucified, he spent a night celebrating the Passover feast with his disciples. This special meal was a commemoration of that time I sent the death angle to kill the first born of the Egyptians in order to set my people free. As you celebrate meals with your family may you be reminded of that first Passover. I am still passing over you not with a curse, but with a blessing. I am hovering over you with my covering, my love, my joy, my faith, my will, my understanding, my truth, my peace, and my long-suffering. As you prepare to go forth as a servant, remember that I will always be with you to the very end.

Scriptures for today: Matt. 28: 19-20
Therefore go and make disciples of all

*nations, baptizing them in the name of the
Father and of the Son and of the Holy
Spirit, 20 and teaching them to obey
everything I have commanded you. And
surely, I am with you always, to the very end
of the age."*
Acts 1:8 *But you will receive power when the
Holy Spirit comes on you; and you will be my
witnesses in Jerusalem, and in all Judea and
Samaria, and to the ends of the earth."*

God, I hear you:

_____

_____

_____

_____

_____

_____

_____

_____

_____

_____

_____

_____

_____

_____

_____

_____

_____

Day 36   A New Message

As you have sat quietly these days, I have shared so much with you. I know you have been spiritually fed from my truth. You have searched my word and now they are real in your soul. You are real and ready to share that new message from your heart. Every word that comes from your mouth are now my words. You now know what so many of my children have yet to learn. You walk in abundance experience a foretaste of heaven.

I suppose who want to know what's next? What do you do with this mind filled with wonder and expectations? As I sent Jesus, I am also sending you to bring this message to those struggling and hurting unnecessary because of sin. I want the world to know me and the fullness of my power in their lives. I want others in the family to mature in the faith so they can also live abundantly. Just as I have given you a new message, I will provide the time and place for you to share. I want you to commit your voice to wherever I lead you. Do not be afraid, keep your eyes focused on me and move by my spirit.

Scriptures for today: Esther 4:14 *For if you remain silent at this time, relief and deliverance for the Jews will arise from another place, but you and your father's family will perish. And who knows but that you have come to your royal position for such a time as this?"*
Isa. 58:1 *Cry aloud, spare not; Lift up your voice like a trumpet(NKJV)*
Mark 12:30 *Love the Lord your God with all your heart and with all your soul and with all your mind and with all your strength.'*

God, I hear you:

_____
_____
_____
_____
_____
_____
_____
_____
_____
_____
_____

Day 37   *Strange Feelings*

I can only imagine that you must be wondering what your friends will think when you share that you have actually spent 40 days in silence listening to God. Maybe some won't believe you or perhaps you are experimenting with a new religion. You may have strange feelings about this experience

When we began, I shared with you that this was all in my plan for you. I wanted you to know the fullness of my presence and to experience intimacy with me as LORD. There are many battles ahead and I wanted you to be prepared like a soldier graduating from boot camp. In this world you are called to defend my truth to those who are lost. I have a special place that needs your message.

As you mature in the faith you will understand how special this time has been. Don't feel that this experience will end, for I will continue to communicate with you. I will always have a word for you. Just be patient and keep on believing.

Scriptures for today: Isa 40:31 But those who wait on the LORD
Shall renew their strength; They shall mount up with wings like eagles, they shall run and not be weary, they shall walk and not faint.(NKJV)
2Tim. 1:12 for I know whom I have believed and am persuaded that He is able to keep what I have committed to Him until that Day (NKJV)

God, I hear you:

_____
_____
_____
_____
_____
_____
_____
_____
_____
_____
_____
_____
_____
_____
_____
_____
_____

Day 38   The Greatest Love

I showed my love when I came to live among the people on the earth, As I walked on the earth, I knew I was to become the perfect sacrifice for the sins of the world. My love was greater than any love man could ever imagine. Because of you, many of my children will know of this amazing love. Each day my love for you grows and grows and I want you to reach out and share this love with those who need to know me. Look beyond, race, color, nationality, economic status, even religion for people need to know ME! Look pass their faults or those who are unlovable and allow me to love through you. Remember you are the only Bible they will ever read.

Perhaps you are feeling unloved in your marriage, at work, or even at church, but I want you to know that I LOVE YOU. As you sit and listen today feel my strong arms surrounding you. My love for you will never change.

Scriptures for today: John 15:13
Greater love has no one than this: to lay down one's life for one's friends.
Luke 10:27 *'Love the Lord your God with all your heart and with all your soul and with all your strength and with all your mind'; and, 'Love your neighbor as yourself.*

God, I hear you:

_____
_____
_____
_____
_____
_____
_____
_____
_____
_____
_____
_____
_____
_____
_____
_____
_____
_____

Day 39   *Silly*

I know you have endured many
attacks from the enemy and even
thought you were silly for spending this
time in silence with me. It is his job to
discourage you and convince you this is
all foolishness. The enemy's strong
words are beginning to make sense
when you ponder over them in your
natural mind. Perhaps in your mind you
felt like you have wasted your time.
Maybe you have shared with another
friend and they tried to discourage you.
It doesn't take all this to be a Christian,
or does it?

Before you became a believer, I
loved you jealously and offered your
salvation while you were yet in your
sins. It was your choice to accept my Son
as Savior granting you eternal life, but
there's so much more. My purpose in
coming to the earth was more than
salvation. I came to give you a life filled
with blessings and a taste of heaven on
earth. I want you to experience the
fullness of my presence and making me
LORD of your life. I don't want you to be
a survivor, I want you to be an over-

comer. I want you to LIVE!!! And live a life more abundantly. "In your face satan," for this child you call silly, belongs to me.

Scriptures for today: Jude 24 *To him who is able to keep you from stumbling and to present you before his glorious presence without fault and with great joy—*
Phil. 1:6 *being confident of this, that he who began a good work in you will carry it on to completion until the day of Christ Jesus.*

God, I hear you:

_____
_____
_____
_____
_____
_____
_____
_____
_____
_____
_____
_____

Day 40   *What Ya Say*

Well, I have been surprised and honored that you would allow me to take to you these 40 days. I've said so much, and you have listened. We have grown closer and closer and I know this will not be our last encounter. I hope you have learned that prayer is conversational and there will be times I need to say something to you. Being silent the 40 days have given you a lot to say. I want you to tell it wherever you go. Remember I love you and will always be with you even when you won't let me say a word. As you go, I'm rejoicing because you are MINE!!!!

Scriptures for today: 1Cor. 15:58
Therefore, my beloved brethren, be steadfast, immovable, always abounding in the work of the Lord, knowing that your labor is not in vain in the Lord.
Heb. 6: 10-11 For God is not unjust to forget your work and [10]labor of love which you have shown toward His name, in that you have ministered to the saints, and do minister. [11]And we

desire that each one of you show the same diligence to the full assurance of hope until the end.

God, I hear you:

_____

_____

_____

_____

_____

_____

_____

_____

_____

_____

_____

_____

_____

_____

_____

_____

_____

_____

_____

From my heart:

EPILOGUE

My God what a word!!! Glory to God and what a wonderful change that has come over me. God has spoken to my heart these past 40 days in ways I never expected. I assumed this writing would be just a simple prayer journal for the mission group. We would pray through the 40 days, share with each other, and put it away. God spoke to me revealing things I needed to know. Many days I sat weeping as God revealed my imperfections, and days I was so filled with His Presence inside heaven's door. My spirit was strengthened so much that satan was like a whipped dog. I danced through every storm as I experienced a sweet fellowship I had never known.

After the mission trip the group came together and discovered God had indeed done a new thing in us. My sisters encouraged me to get the journal published so other could experience being along in His presence.

As you journey through this experience, expect to be changed, challenged, and chastised. Your experience won't be the same and someone else for you are unique in God's eyes. If you will sit in silence for whatever amount of time you decide, God will speak. This is not a journal for new believers, but rather for seasoned saints who are ready for the next level. It's my prayer that you will also grow into intimacy with Him and that you will experience the abundant life God promised to all his children.

With Jesus Love.

MS. CHOCOLATE

GWEN "MS. CHOCOLATE" WILLIAMS
Author, Motivational Speaker,
Folklorist

Gwen grew up in Alexandria, Louisiana on a small chicken farm with her parents and older brother. She got a strong foundation from her teachers at the J. B. LaFargue elementary school. All of her teachers at Peabody Senior High school thought Gwen majored in extra-curricular activities. When she graduated in 1965 Gwen thought she would enter college to major in Nursing, but God stepped in and she earned a BA in Applied Music from the University of Southwestern Louisiana.

Gwen began her missionary journey in the inner-city of Detroit, Michigan. She continued her education at the New Orleans Baptist Theological Seminary earning a master's degree in Church Music. After serving for nearly fifteen years with the Southern Baptist Convention, Gwen was called by God to start her own ministry. In 1992 she formed From the Heart Ministries. Through this ministry she developed her career as a storyteller and writer.

Gwen started writing poetry, but soon discovered she could write stories. Her first writing assignment was a favorite Christmas story that was published in the Times Picayune of New Orleans Louisiana. She has written Sunday School, Training Union and Mission literature. She has shared her stories with many schools throughout the country and in Canada

93

to boost self-worth and self-esteem. She is the author of a series of children books: Effie and his encouraging F-words. "Been Cross de Tracks is her most recent publication depicting her journey from Louisiana to Mississippi and many points along the way.

For scheduling and/or product information, write or call

Gwen Williams

136 Veronica Drive, Picayune, MS. 39466

(601) 798-3548

chocolatelavern@yahoo

For additional copies:

Order from: Amazon.com or from
Gwen Williams

Made in United States
North Haven, CT
06 May 2023

36311993R00055